HOW? WHO? WHAT? WHEN? WHERE? WHY?

Questions kids ask

ABOUT
INSECTS AND SPIDERS

PUBLISHER	Joseph R. DeVarennes	
PUBLICATION DIRECTOR	Kenneth H. Pearson	
ADVISORS	Roger Aubin	
	Robert Furlonger	
EDITORIAL SUPERVISOR	Jocelyn Smyth	
PRODUCTION MANAGER	Ernest Homewood	
PRODUCTION ASSISTANTS	Martine Gingras	Kathy Kishimoto
	Catherine Gordon	Peter Thomlison
CONTRIBUTORS	Alison Dickie	Nancy Prasad
	Bill Ivy	Lois Rock
	Jacqueline Kendel	Merebeth Switzer
	Anne Langdon	Dave Taylor
	Sheila Macdonald	Alison Tharen
	Susan Marshall	Donna Thomson
	Pamela Martin	Pam Young
	Colin McCance	
SENIOR EDITOR	Robin Rivers	
EDITORS	Brian Cross	Ann Martin
	Anne Louise Mahoney	Mayta Tannenbaum
PUBLICATION ADMINISTRATOR	Anna Good	
ART AND DESIGN	Richard Comely	Ronald Migliore
	Robert B. Curry	Penelope Moir
	George Elliott	Marion Stuck
	Marilyn James	Bill Suddick
	Robert Johanssen	Sue Wilkinson

Canadian Cataloguing in Publication Data

Main entry under title:

Questions kids ask about insects and spiders

(Questions kids ask ; 11)
ISBN 0-7172-2550-X

1. Insects—Miscellanea—Juvenile literature.
2. Spiders—Miscellanea—Juvenile literature.
3. Children's questions and answers. I. Smyth, Jocelyn.
II. Comely, Richard.   III. Series.

QL467.2.Q47 1988   j595.7   C89-093163-1

Questions Kids Ask . . . about INSECTS AND SPIDERS

continued

What is an insect?

To many people any small creepy crawly creature is an insect. However, to really qualify as an insect an animal must have six legs and a body which is divided into three parts.

Insects come in all sizes, shapes and colors. Some have wings and two feelers or antennae; others do not. One common feature is a hard outer body casing known as an exoskeleton. Also of interest are their unique eyes which may contain 28 000 individual lenses! Although some insects cannot hear, they can see, smell and taste. Butterflies, moths, beetles, bees and ants are just a few of the more common members members of this incredible animal class.

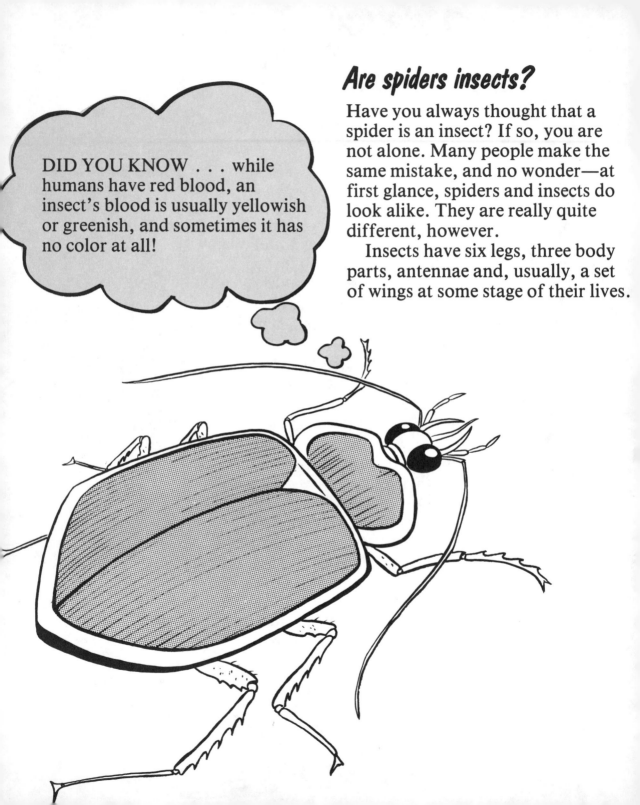

Are spiders insects?

Have you always thought that a spider is an insect? If so, you are not alone. Many people make the same mistake, and no wonder—at first glance, spiders and insects do look alike. They are really quite different, however.

Insects have six legs, three body parts, antennae and, usually, a set of wings at some stage of their lives.

DID YOU KNOW . . . while humans have red blood, an insect's blood is usually yellowish or greenish, and sometimes it has no color at all!

Spiders, on the other hand, have eight legs and only two body parts. They never have wings or antennae, though they do have a pair of feelers, known as *palpi,* that look like two short legs.

Spiders belong to a class of animals known as Arachnids. Scorpions, mites and ticks are also members of this class.

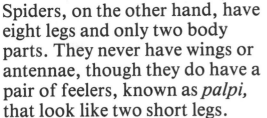

DID YOU KNOW . . . the black widow spider certainly has earned its name. It is not uncommon for the female spider to kill and eat her partner after mating.

Why do bees buzz?

As the honeybee flies from flower to flower you hear its distinctive humming bzzzzzz . . . The bee isn't humming its favorite tune. The sound is made by the bee's wings. A bee moves its tiny wings very quickly when it flies—a busy bee can fly as far as 19 kilometres (12 miles) in one hour. What we hear is actually the rapid beating of the bee's wings.

DID YOU KNOW . . . a bee can fly forward, sideways or backward, and can hover in one place.

Is a bee sting dangerous?

Have you ever been stung by a bee? If you have then you already know how much it can hurt! Luckily, for most of us a bee sting is not really dangerous. After a short time the pain goes away and the swelling around the sting goes down. However, for a few people, a bee sting can be deadly. These people are very allergic to bee stings and react so violently that they must get medical help immediately or they may die. Although most of us are fortunate enough not to be afflicted with this frightful allergy, it is best to leave bees alone—because then they will leave you alone.

How do honeybees keep warm in winter?

Many insects die when cold weather sets in, but honeybees live through the winter and into the following spring. These fascinating creatures aren't physically equipped to withstand the cold better than any other insects. But when it comes to keeping warm, honeybees are smart. They use a clever cooperative system to stay warm all through the winter.

The bees cluster together in the hive and keep their wings and bodies moving in a sort of dance to generate heat. They take turns resting, and at intervals they change places so that the bees on the outside can have their turn in the center, where it is warmest. By feeding on stored supplies and sharing body heat, these energetic workers can protect themselves from the bitterest cold. So, honeybees are not only busy bees in summer, they are busy all winter long!

What is the biggest insect in the world?

This depends on what you mean by "biggest"—is it the longest, the heaviest or the biggest around? The longest insect in the world is the walkingstick. Walkingsticks are long and thin. They look and even act like twigs because they lie very still for hours. Some are quite small, but those that live in the tropics can be up to 38 centimetres (15 inches) long.

The really big insects, however, are all beetles. One, called the rhinoceros beetle because it has horns, is quite large and rather fearsome. But the Hercules and Goliath beetles are even bigger. The Hercules can measure 18 centimetres (7 inches) in length. The Goliath, although shorter, is equipped with thick armor and is therefore heavier. It weighs about 100 grams (3-1/2 ounces).

Some butterflies and moths are also quite large, marrying size with beauty. The most amazing is a moth in Australia that has a wingspread of 36 centimetres (14 inches). This moth has often been mistaken for a bird!

DID YOU KNOW . . . a beetle can lift 750 times its own weight!

How many kinds of insects are there?

There is certainly no shortage of insects in the world. In fact, there are more species of insects than of any other animal. Incredibly, a couple of square kilometres (a square mile) of land may contain as many insects as there are people in the world! Close to one million species are already known and more are being discovered each year. Some scientists believe that as many as two million have yet to be identified. So the next time you see an insect you don't recognize, look closely—it just might be a new discovery!

Which insect has the largest appetite?

When it comes to eating, no creature in all of nature can compete with the larva of the Polyphemus moth. This miniature eating machine feeds on leaves day and night, stopping only briefly to rest between meals. During the first two days of its life it consumes an incredible 86 000 times its own birthweight in food! To match this feat an average baby would have to eat 300 metric tons of pablum.

DID YOU KNOW . . . one beetle has a stomach that must be made of iron. It not only likes hot red pepper but as many as 45 drugs and poisons are on its menu as well. No wonder it is called the ''drugstore'' beetle! And, believe it or not, it has a close relative that likes to eat strong cigars.

How do spiders build webs?

Spider webs come in a variety of shapes and sizes. Many of them are quite beautiful. A spider spins its web from liquid silk manufactured by six glands in its body. This silk flows through *spinnerets,* tiny tubes like nozzles that are located below the abdomen on the underside of the spider. Strands of silk are drawn from the spinnerets by the claws on the spider's feet and the threads are then attached to a tree or plant to form a pattern unique to each species. Some threads in the web are sticky and others are not, but the spider always knows which is which. However, should the spider miss its step, it has extra protection—its feet are equipped with a slippery oil to prevent it from being caught in its own trap.

How is silk made?

Silk is one of the finest fabrics used for clothing. A silk shirt or dress is something most anyone would prize.

Much of the fabric made today is synthetic; scientists have used chemicals to make it. But silk is made by an insect—the silkworm, to be exact. The silkworm is actually the caterpillar of a moth that originally lived only in the Far East.

In early summer, the female moth lays between 300 and 500 eggs. These are collected by silk farmers and left in a cool place for the winter. When spring comes, they hatch into tiny caterpillars, or silkworms. The silkworms eat continuously until they grow to their full length of about 8 centimetres (3 inches). Then they begin to spin their cocoons, the wrappings of silk thread in which they will develop into adult moths.

On silk farms, only a few of the caterpillars are allowed to live once the cocoon is finished. If the moth emerges from the cocoon, the pure silk thread will be broken. In most cases, therefore, the insects are killed inside the cocoons and the cocoons are put into water. When the silk threads begin to unravel, the ends are caught and wound onto reels.

DID YOU KNOW . . . 25 000 cocoons are needed to make 450 grams (1 pound) of silk.

How high can a flea jump?

Fleas—the tiny biting insects that pester our pet cats and dogs—are incredible high jumpers. A flea can jump 130 times its height. Kangaroos, which are considered the best jumpers of the mammal world, only leap four times their height. If you could jump as well as a flea you would be able to jump up to the top of a 50-storey building!

DID YOU KNOW . . . an insect's eye is really made up of thousands of small eyes—the dragonfly has 15 000!

Can a housefly be deadly?

Houseflies do not bite or carry any poison. They are tiny little featherweights, so they can't knock you down and trample you. Therefore, pesky as they are, they must be basically harmless. Right? Wrong. Houseflies can be very dangerous. You have probably seen a housefly walk upside down across the ceiling. To accomplish this amazing trick the fly has a set of sticky pads covering its feet. These sticky feet pick up germs. Houseflies can be deadly because they can carry disease.

Can a fly kill a horse?

You would think that horses could kill any fly that came too close for comfort with one swish of their tails. But certain kinds of flies *can* kill a horse. They're called horse bots, throat bots and nose bots.

The female botfly lays eggs on the hair of the horse's legs, nose or lips. The horse licks at the eggs, and as they hatch, swallows them. The larvae travel to the horse's stomach and feed on tissues and fluid there. If too many botfly larvae reach its stomach, the horse will die. Certain medicines can kill botflies, but the horse must be treated before too much damage has already been done in order to save its life.

DID YOU KNOW . . . fireflies use their light as a mating signal. The males dance above the ground and flash their lights at females waiting in the grass. Interested females flash back to let the males know where they are.

How does a firefly make its light?

Fireflies are not flies. Fireflies are beetles! One of nature's wonders, they glow like flickering sparks of fire in the dark. How do they do it?

Their outer bodies are composed of three layers, each contributing in its own way to this production of light. The inner layer is made of cells that act as reflectors, or mirrors to make the light more brilliant. The middle layer contains cells that actually produce the light. These cells are made up of a very complex group of chemicals. And the outer layer, the firefly's skin, is transparent—like a window, which allows the light to shine through. But the middle layer does most of the work. At a signal from the firefly's nervous system, a chemical called pyrophosphate is released and it combines with oxygen and five other chemicals to cause flashes of light in the sides of the firefly's body. Seconds later, another chemical is released, causing the light to go out.

How do worms get into apples?

Did you know that the worms found in apples actually live there? Most of these worms come from the codling moth, which is known to be extremely destructive to apple orchards.

Its larva, the appleworm, hibernates in a cocoon over the winter on the bark of apple trees. The adult moth emerges in the spring and lays transparent eggs on the leaves of the apple. The eggs hatch into little caterpillars that burrow into the ripening fruit, where they happily munch away.

If not picked, the apples fall from the trees in autumn and the larvae crawl out of the apples and take their turn to hibernate. The following spring, there they are—adult moths laying their eggs on the new apple leaves, and the cycle starts all over again.

Why do moths eat wool?

Have you ever pulled your winter clothes out of storage and found holes eaten into the wool? "Those moths have been at it again," your parents probably complain.

Actually, not all moths eat wool. It is only the clothes moth species that is a problem. And you can't even blame the winged adult moths that you may see occasionally in your home. Why? Because it is the young larvae, or caterpillars, of the moths that do the damage. They eat wool and other materials, especially those that are greasy or sweaty. So,

how do the caterpillars get on the wool in the first place?

The female adult moths lay their eggs on wool and other fabrics. When the eggs develop into larvae, the larvae begin eating the first thing they find—the material they are living on. As for the adults, not only do they not eat wool—they don't eat at all!

DID YOU KNOW . . . the caterpillar of the Io moth has poisonous spines on its body to protect it from enemies.

What animals hunt spiders?

Life for a spider is full of
danger. It has many enemies to
be on the alert for. Birds,
mammals, reptiles, amphibians
and fish all enjoy spiders for
lunch. No creature can be
trusted, not even its own kind.
But the most deadly enemies of
all are the tiny flies and wasps
that lay their eggs in or on the
spider's body. Once the eggs
hatch, the grubs begin to eat
their hosts—not a very pleasant
situation for the spider. The
hunter has become the hunted.

Are tarantulas dangerous?

Few creatures are as unpopular as the tarantula. Just the thought of these large, hairy spiders makes many people shudder. However, looks are deceiving. Far from being the villains portrayed in films and books, tarantulas are actually very timid animals. The bite of North American tarantulas is no more dangerous than that of a bee. Although the bite of some South American species can be hazardous, they never attack people unless provoked. When cornered, a tarantula usually lets you know it is frightened by rearing up on its hind legs and making a strange purring sound before striking.

Most tarantulas are ground-dwelling spiders which sleep in a burrow during the day. A few live in trees and can grow quite large. One South American species, known as the bird-eating spider, has a body 9 centimetres (3-1/2 inches) long and a leg span of 18 centimetres (7 inches). True to its name it has been known to eat baby birds!

DID YOU KNOW . . . one species of spider can run 33 times its body length per second!

How can an ant tell a friend from an enemy?

Look closely at an ant. Now look at another . . . and another . . . and another. All of them look pretty much alike, don't they? So how can an ant from one nest recognize another ant from the same nest?

Ants have a pair of sensitive feelers called antennae on the top of their heads. They use their antennae to touch objects, and in this way to identify and measure them. An ant can both smell and taste using its antennae. Soldier ants guard the entrance to an ant nest. Each ant that wants to enter the nest is inspected by a soldier's antennae. Since all the ants from one nest smell the same, the soldier can tell by the smell of the ant whether it belongs to the nest or should be sent away.

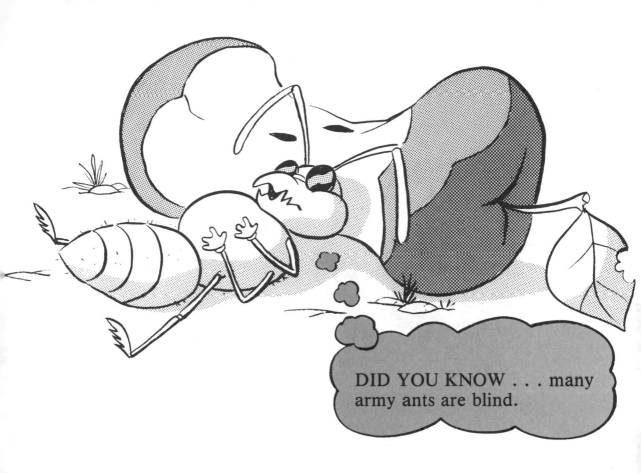

DID YOU KNOW . . . many army ants are blind.

Are army ants dangerous?

Army ants are not really a threat to people but to many animals they certainly are! They move forward in dense ranks, often 3 to 4 metres (9 to 12 feet) wide and can travel up to 33 kilometres (20 miles) per hour. There may be as many as one million ants in a single column and each one has sharp jaws and a large appetite. All living creatures flee in terror before the marching horde because these hungry hunters will devour any creature that gets in their way. Sick or injured animals are therefore at greater risk because they are not always able to escape in time. Believe it or not, army ants can strip an elephant to the bone or pick a horse clean in hours.

Where do insects go in winter?

While you may not see many insects in winter, there are more around than you think—you just have to look a little harder to find them. Although many have a very short life and die before winter, others find a way to survive during the cold weather.

A large number of insects pass the winter in the form of eggs, protected by a sac around them.

Others winter as larvae, little caterpillars quietly sleeping in silk cocoons or in sheltered nests made of leaves. Some bugs and beetles are active all winter long while others, such as leaf beetles, hibernate in the bark of trees or under leaves. Some aquatic nymphs hibernate too, but other water bugs are busy scurrying around under the ice during the cold season.

Honeybees huddle together in the hive, keeping their wings and bodies in constant motion to keep the hive warm. Most butterflies winter as a pupa, a resting stage in which they lie very still in a case and change from a caterpillar into a beautiful butterfly. But not all insects stay to brave the cold—a few, like the monarch butterfly, fly long distances to spend the winter in the sunny south.

Do all insects fly?

Only three groups of animals can fly under their own power: bats, birds and insects. Insects are the oldest of the flying animals.

Insect fossils that looked just like dragonflies have been found in 300 million-year-old rock!

Most adult insects have two pairs of wings. The hard outer wings protect the more fragile inner ones. Each type of insect flies at a different rate: butterflies beat their wings 4 to 20 times per second, bees 100 times per second and mosquitoes an incredible 1000 times per second. The fastest ~~flier~~ is the dragonfly with a speed of 56 kilometres (35 miles) per hour.

Yet not all insects have wings. Most ants are wingless. Some insects must rely on strong legs to run after prey and to make speedy get-aways. Other insects only possess wings for a short time. Female scale insects can fly until they find a good place to live. The wings of queen ants fall off after they finish mating.

So don't be surprised if you see an insect without wings.

DID YOU KNOW . . . one migration of painted lady butterflies was so massive that it was 60 kilometres (about 40 miles) wide. It took three days for them to pass a given spot.

Why does a caterpillar shed its skin?

A baby butterfly looks nothing like its beautiful parents. It is shaped like a chubby worm, and it is called a caterpillar. Caterpillars spend almost all of their time eating. Each kind of caterpillar has a special type of food which it loves to eat. All of this eating makes them grow and grow and grow.

Soon the caterpillar becomes too big for its skin, which splits down the back. Underneath is a new layer that is big enough for the caterpillar to grow into. A caterpillar may go through four or five shedding periods before it becomes a pupa and changes into a butterfly.

Why are moths attracted to light?

Like many insects, moths are irresistibly drawn to light. You often see groups of them circling a lighted patio or a street lamp.

In the wild, moths navigate by the light of the moon and the stars, which are so far away that their rays of light are almost parallel to each other by the time they reach the earth. Moths use these rays to direct their flight. They fly with the rays always striking their eyes at the same angle.

But artificial light creates a problem for the moth because the rays from this type of light are not parallel. In order to keep the light striking its eye at the same angle the moth must keep turning. Approaching closer and closer, the confused moth eventually spirals into the light.

How did the praying mantis get its name?

If you have ever seen a praying mantis you probably already know how it got its name. While at rest this peaceful-looking insect holds its front legs up as though they are joined in prayer. But the appearance of the mantis is deceiving. It is a truly savage creature, and it is not praying—it is waiting for its dinner to arrive.

Perched in this manner it sits motionless until an unsuspecting insect passes by. Then, with lightning speed, it reaches out and grabs its doomed victim. Unable to free itself from the deadly clutch of the spike-lined legs, the insect is promptly eaten. On second thought, the praying mantis may be praying after all—it may be saying grace!

DID YOU KNOW . . . the praying mantis is one of the few insects that can turn its head.

Why do mosquito bites itch?

The mosquito is probably the most unpopular flying insect in the world. Not only can its bite spread disease, it can be extremely irritating. After penetrating your skin with her needle-sharp beak the female mosquito draws up your blood. She has a special substance in her saliva to prevent the blood from clotting. If you are allergic to this liquid as most people are, the bite will swell and itch. A few lucky individuals are not bothered at all by mosquito bites.

Why do bees sting?

Some people think that bees sting because they are nasty. This isn't true. A bee will only sting if it is caught or hurt or if it feels that the hive is in danger. The main threat comes from animals that want to get at the sweet honey inside the hive.

A bee sting hurts you, but it will probably kill the bee. The bee's tiny stinger gets hooked so firmly in your skin that the bee tears its body when it tries to fly away. The bee dies after losing its stinger.

Why are wasps so pesky in late summer?

It is the last long weekend of the summer, and you are at a picnic. The hamburgers are sizzling on the barbecue and everything is fine until *they* show up. *They* are yellow jacket wasps.

In the spring, the queen wasp built a nest and began laying eggs. At first she laid only a few because she was all alone to feed the grub-like larvae when they hatched. Soon they grew into adult worker wasps, and took over feeding the new larvae. From then on, all the queen did was lay eggs.

For a while, life was easy as new flowers and insects increased the food supply. But the colony has been getting bigger all summer long. By late August it may contain as many as 5000 wasps. The natural food supply is dwindling and the wasps are on the lookout for food. Your picnic is just what they need. It has sweets (catsup and mustard) for the wasps themselves, and meat for the larvae.

DID YOU KNOW . . . bees from a single hive may visit 250 000 flowers in one day!

Can spiders fly?

What has eight legs, no wings and flies? Believe it or not it's a spider.

Baby spiders, or spiderlings, fly by a method known as ballooning. First they climb up as high as possible on a plant or fence post to prepare for take-off. Turning to face the wind they spin one or more long strands of silk known as gossamer from their abdomen. The wind catches the silk and, like a kite, the lightweight spiderlings are carried high into the air. Few travel very far, but some may journey great distances. Pilots have reported seeing these little astronauts flying as high as 4300 metres (14 000 feet). Others have been seen 300 kilometres (200 miles) out at sea.

Once the spiderlings touch down, they discard their parachutes and explore their new surroundings. If they are not happy with them, they soar off once again in search of a better home.

Do all spiders spin webs?

While all spiders produce silk, not all of them spin webs. Those that don't must rely on their hunting rather than trapping skills to catch their food. Some, like the tarantula and the wolf spider, hunt on the ground and stalk their prey. Others, like the crab spider, sit on flowers quietly waiting for an insect to drop by for a visit—and then quickly snatch it up. Jumping spiders creep around, looking for an insect to pounce on, and water spiders hunt underwater.

But the most unusual of all hunting spiders is the bola spider. It produces a dangling silk thread with a sticky ball at

DID YOU KNOW . . . a spider can spin a line so fine that it is invisible to the human eye, or it can spin one heavy enough to snare snakes, birds and mice.

the end. When a moth flies by it throws this "lasso" into the air and snares its victim's wings and legs. The spider then simply crawls along the line, eats the trapped moth—and feels very pleased with itself!

Index _____